The Reason for the Season

INTRODUCTION

Children dream of jingle bells, Rudolf-the-Red-Nosed-Reindeer, Kris Kringle, bright colored lights, candy canes, and presents under the tree. Eyes sparkle at the first sign of the upcoming holiday season.

Adults dream, too, with every Christmas card we write, sending happy greetings to those we care about. With all the commercialism, excitement, and hurry of the season, we sometimes forget the season's reason. This book will help you feel the mystery and wonder of it all.

Each essay shows the season's true meaning with appropriate Bible passages taken from the New International Version of the Holy Bible, the history behind each story, and customs associated with the event. Read through this book, meditate, pray, and celebrate the birth of our Lord and Savior, Jesus Christ, once again. Amaze yourself with the wonder of Mary's courage, the faith of Joseph, and the glory of God.

—Margaret "Peggy" Best

The Reason for the Season
Bible Verses, Devotions, Personal Essays, Crafts, & Prayers
MARGARET BEST

Margaret Best prefers her nick-name, *Peggy*.

After retiring from teaching elementary school, Peggy lived her dream of becoming a writer. After several years in training, she published her first book *Unsung Hero* in 2018. Astonished, she won a medal for the book.

She wrote her second, *Dandelion Child: A Soldier's Daughter*, in 2019 and won a second award. She ghost wrote the book *Doris Vail: Navy Trailblazer* in 2020. All three books are memoirs, one of her father, the other of herself as a child, and the third of a female retired naval officer.

As an Army Brat and the wife of a company engineer, Peggy traveled often, lived in foreign countries, and explored different cultures. One of her passions was studying various cultures, their traditions, and religion.

Peggy lives in a retirement community in Florida with her husband of over fifty years. Her three grown children visit often with her eight grandchildren. Everywhere Peggy travels her first order of business is to find a church. She is a Christian, who reads the Bible, rarely argues, and always prays.

The Reason for The Season, Peggy's first published book of devotional essays, helps people better understand why we celebrate Christmas. Three circumstances brought this book about.

The first was a visit from a Realtor who had written a devotional book when he suffered from depression. After reading it, Peggy decided she could write one too.

The second was her visit with a surgeon who informed her she needed knee surgery. Due to the Covid-19 Pandemic of 2020-2021, she became home bound.

The third was a phone call from a pastor. Instead of attending church services, she spent her time reading the Bible, researching on the internet, praying, and receiving insight to share with others.

The Reason for The Season is the culmination of her efforts. She wrote an essay almost every day and gathered her Christmas essays. After thought, prayer, and discussion she decided they are worth sharing with the public.

"My hope is this book will become a means to help churches or other organizations raise funds and help people marvel at the reason for the season—the birth of our Savior," Peggy says.

The Reason for the Season

ISBN: 978-1-951188-36-8

Bulk personalized copies of *The Reason for the Season* are available at discounted rates for churches and organizations to use as fund raisers and gifts for donations.

For further information visit

www.MargaretBestAuthor.com/My-Books.com

HALLARD PRESS

3070 Collins Court
The Villages, FL 32163
352-234-6099
www.HallardPress.com

TABLE OF CONTENTS

Joy to the world

During the time of Christmas, most Christians display a nativity scene similar to the one above. I present the following pages as I ponder the Bible's words, with the hope that you, too, will experience the wonder of our Savior's birth.

Jesus' disciples wrote the story below, found in The International Version of the New Testament in the Bible.

The Birth of Jesus

Luke Chapter 2: 1-22

In those days, Caesar Augustus issued a decree that a census should be taken of the entire Roman world. (This was the first census that took place while Quirinius was governor of Syria.) And everyone went to their own town to register.

So Joseph also went up from the town of Nazareth in Galilee to Judea, to Bethlehem the town of David, because he belonged to the house and line of David. He went there to register with Mary, who was pledged to be married to him and was expecting a child. While they were there, the time came for the baby to be born, and she gave birth to her firstborn, a son. She wrapped him in cloths and placed him in a manger because there was no guest room available for them.

And there were shepherds living out in the fields nearby, keeping watch over their flocks at night. An angel of the Lord appeared to them, and the glory of the Lord shone around them, and they were terrified.

But the angel said to them, "Do not be afraid. I bring you good news that will cause great joy for all the people. Today in the town of David, a Savior has been born to you; he is the Messiah, the Lord. This will be a sign to you: You will find a baby wrapped in cloths and lying in a manger."

Suddenly a great company of the heavenly host appeared with the angel, praising God and saying, "Glory to God in the highest heaven, and on earth peace to those on whom his favor rests."

When the angels had left them and gone into heaven, the shepherds said to one another, "Let's go to Bethlehem and see this thing that has happened, which the Lord has told us about."

So they hurried off and found Mary and Joseph, and the baby, who was lying in the manger. When they had seen him, they spread the word concerning what had been told them about this child, and all who heard it were amazed at what the shepherds said to them. But Mary treasured up all these things and pondered them in her heart.

The shepherds returned, glorifying and praising God for all the things they had heard and seen, which were just as they had been told.

On the eighth day, when it was time to circumcise the child, he was named Jesus, the name the angel had given him before he was conceived.

The Wise Men Visit

Mathew 2:1-12

After Jesus was born in Bethlehem in Judea, during the time of King Herod, Magi from the east came to Jerusalem and asked, "Where is the one who has been born king of the Jews? We saw his star when it rose and have come to worship him."

When King Herod heard this, he was disturbed, and all Jerusalem with him. When he had called together all the people's chief priests and teachers of the law, he asked them where the Messiah was to be born. "In Bethlehem in Judea," they replied, "for this is what the prophet has written: " 'But you, Bethlehem, in the land of Judah, are by no means least among the rulers of Judah; for out of you will come a ruler who will shepherd my people Israel.' "

Then Herod called the Magi secretly and found out from them the exact time the star had appeared. He sent them to Bethlehem and said, "Go and search carefully for the child. As soon as you find him, report to me so that I too may go and worship him."

After they had heard the king, they went on their way, and the star they had seen when it rose went ahead of them until it stopped over the place where the child was. When they saw the star, they were overjoyed. On coming to the house, they saw the child with his mother Mary, and they bowed down and worshiped him. Then they opened their treasures and presented him with gifts of gold, frankincense, and myrrh.

And having been warned in a dream not to go back to Herod, they returned to their country by another route.

The Season of Christmas Advent

O Come, O Come Emmanuel, And ransom captive Israel...

What is the Christmas Season all about?

Children in most Western-oriented countries think of the Christmas Season is a time out of school, Santa Claus, and presents under the Christmas tree.

Is that all there is to the season?

Christmas is a distinctively Christian holiday celebrated in different ways in different cultures and countries. Christianity has by far the most significant percentage of adherents of any religion on earth.

Greek Orthodox and Eastern Catholics observe a 40-day fast from November 15 in preparation for the Christmas celebration. Western Christianity, especially the Roman Catholic Church, celebrates from the fourth Sunday before Christmas through Christmas Eve, called the Advent Season.

What is Advent Season?

Advent, when western Christians prepare for the coming of the Messiah and the celebration of Christmas, begins on the fourth Sunday before Christmas or the closest Sunday to St. Andrew's Day, which falls on November 30 each year, and ends on Christmas Day. The official beginning of the custom of Advent is obscure. However, Roman Catholic monks began fasting on December 1 through Christmas day at the Second Council of Tours in 567 AD.

What are the traditional customs of Advent?

Every year my family purchases an **Advent Calendar**. The children open one window on the calendar each day for four weeks before Christmas. They find a piece of Christmas candy or a small toy.

We also make or purchase an **Advent Wreath** for use as a table decoration. The **Advent Wreath** first appeared in Germany in 1869. A Lutheran minister working at a mission for children created a wreath out of a cart's wheel. He placed twenty small red candles and four large white candles inside the ring. The children lit the red candles on weekdays and the four white candles on Sundays.

Today, many churches display an **Advent Wreath** containing five candles to symbolize several sacred phases of preparation. The three Advent candle colors are purple, pink, and white. In the first week, we light the purple candle of hope. We light the purple candle of peace on the second week, and on the third week, the pink candle of Joy, and the fourth week, the purple candle of love. On Christmas Day, the center fifth white candle celebrates Christ's arrival.

To acquaint the children with stories about Jesus, families display a **Jesse Tree.**

Isaiah 11:1: "A shoot shall come out from the stump of Jesse, and a branch shall grow out of his roots."

Jesus descended from the line of David, the greatest king of Israel and the son of Jesse. Jesus is the branch God promised would grow from Jesse's family tree. Each symbol on the tree's ornaments represents a story from within this family tree and a step toward the birth of Jesus. Children read a story about someone in the line of David, then place an ornament or picture of that story on the tree.

How you can celebrate the Season of Advent before Christmas

1. **Create an advent Jesse Tree.** Begin with a small artificial or live tree, cut a tree out of construction paper, and tape it to a wall. Select 24 Bible stories and create small ornaments corresponding with each account. Beginning December 1, read and discuss the related scripture, then place the decoration on the tree. You will find a tool kit for this activity on the Internet at Jesse Tree Symbols and Bible Stories /Faithward.org

2. **Make a Prayer Garland.** Cut out 24 green and red construction paper strips. Write the name of a family member, friend, or ministry on each strip, then staple the strips as links into one long garland. Hang the garland as a decoration. Remove one of the paper strips and pray for that person each day in December.

3. **Make an Advent Wreath.** Purchase an already made wreath ring, candles, and holders from Michaels. Decorate and place the candles around the ring with a large white candle in the center. See the following Internet pages for more designs.

How to Make an Advent Wreath: Quick and Frugal DIY Tutorial—Affording Motherhood (growingslower.com)

How to Make an Advent Wreath in 4 Steps: A Catholic Newbie

Instructions for How to Make an Easy Advent Wreath (learnreligions.com)

4. **Make a family Advent Calendar.** Many YouTube videos are available showing how to make unique calendars or Google free printable advent calendars.

Isaiah 7:14

Therefore the Lord himself will be you a sign: Behold a virgin will be with child and bear a son, and she will call his name Immanuel.

Prayer:
Thank you, Father, for sending your Son to earth in the form of man to forgive our sins and teach love throughout this land. Help us remember this season is not only about toys, food, candy, and family, but mostly about your Savior. In Jesus' name, I pray.

Color the Nativity Scene

Color with fine point markers. An adult/child Christmas activity.

VIRGIN BIRTH

This is how the birth of Jesus Christ came about:

Mathew 1:18
His mother Mary was pledged to be married to Joseph, but before they came together, she was found to be with child through the Holy Spirit.

Sure. Right. Uh Huh.

When I was a little girl, babies came with the stork.

Well, I never saw a stork, but I did see my mother get fat when she was pregnant with my brother.

"We're going to have a baby," she said.

No one explained how we were going to have a baby. It was a mystery. As mommy got bigger and let me feel the baby kicking her tummy, I wondered how the baby got into her stomach. No one explained anything. Then the big day came. We took mommy to the hospital, where she found a baby boy. Did the Holy Spirit make my brother?

Imagine my shock when in fourth-grade health class, the girls watched a film about our menses and how we conceived babies. Gross. Yuck.

I grew up. Five pregnancies and three live babies later, I understand the miracle and love involved in creation. The Holy Spirit has nothing to do with it. Virgins do not have babies.

How am I or you supposed to believe this story in the Bible?

Isaiah 7:14
Therefore, the Lord Himself will give you a sign: Behold a virgin will be with child and bear a son, and she will call His name Immanuel.

There is no logical reason to believe this. There is only faith. I accept and acknowledge that Mary was indeed a virgin with all my heart and soul. Her Son Jesus the Christ is our Savior sent from God to deliver man from his sinful nature and to open life everlasting for us after our human death.

The concept of God makes no sense to those who do not believe.

Let us agree there is a God who is omnipotent and capable of anything. Read the Old Testament to see what Yahweh did for his people, the Jews, then read the New Testament and see what Jesus did. Believe, and see how your faith grows. You will never be alone again, and the story of Christmas will make sense.

Prayer:
Thank you, Lord, for your story of Christmas. Lift the veil of disbelief from the eyes of those who struggle to believe. Help them see the miracle and majesty of your Son, Jesus Christ, during this Christmas season.

Pregnant

Luke 1:38

I am the Lord's servant; Mary answered, "May it be for me as you have said." Then the angel left her.

Imagine what it must have been like for a girl on the cusp of becoming a woman to have an angel appear and announce she was going to carry God's Son. According to custom, young girls between the age of twelve and fourteen accepted arranged marriages. If the girl became pregnant, she would be ostracized, thrown out of her home and the town without any support, or stoned to death.

To believe the angel and carry through was quite a decision for Mary, but she agreed to be a girl of faith. I think the second she said, "May it be for me as you have said," she became pregnant. How? Only God knows, but remember, God can do anything.

I accept all his by faith. There is no logical reasoning behind it.

Mary must have been honored but also frightened. She knew her family, Joseph, and the entire town would not believe the story of an angel. Perhaps she did not believe it herself. Mary must have experienced morning sickness within the first month or so. Duty to attend to her relative Elizabeth, who was quite old and having her first child, took Mary away before her pregnancy showed. Mary stayed with Elizabeth and Zachariah until a few weeks after their Son, John, was born. Mary returned to Nazareth, already showing her pregnancy. Imagine the scene when Mary told Joseph an angel visited her and, even though she remained a virgin, she became pregnant. Imagine the fear she must have experienced. God stepped in. He sent an angel to Joseph. Mary moved in with Joseph, but they did not have relations until after Jesus's birth.

Luke 2:1

In those days, Caesar Augustus issued a decree that a census should be taken of the entire Roman World.

Mary is eight or nine months pregnant. The emperor wants a census so, Joseph and Mary take their donkey several miles away to the town of Bethlehem. They must register there. Traveling today on a train, car, or plane when you are pregnant and ready to pop is not fun. Imagine what it was like for Mary walking and on a donkey. They must have wanted a nice warm bath and bed and breakfast, but there was no room at the inn.

Isaiah 9:6

For unto us a child is born, unto us a son, is given... and his name shall be called Wonderful, Counselor, The Mighty God, The Everlasting Father, The Prince of Peace.

Prayer:
Thank you, Lord, for this gift of your Son as our Savior. Help all those who are pregnant. Send your Angels to them so they will not fear. Allow every child born to be healthy and live a long life. In Jesus' name, I pray.

Angels

Genesis 3:24

After He drove the man out, He placed on the east side of the Garden of Eden cherubim and a flaming sword flashing back and forth to guard the way to the tree of life.

Angels are spirits made by God. The Bible does not give a clear answer to the question: When did God make the angels? However, there is enough evidence to suggest that God made the angels either on the second day after He created heaven or on the third day before He created the earth.

An excellent essay found on https://www.learnreligions.com/ (Fairchild, Mary. "What Does the Bible Say About Angels?") Learn Religions. August 29, 2020, https//www.learnreligions.com/what-does-the-bible-say-about-angels-701965 explains the various types of angels found in the Bible.

Luke 1:28

The Angel went to her and said, "Greetings you who are highly favored. The Lord is with you. You will be with child and give birth to a son, and you are to give him the name Jesus."

One purpose for angels is to take messages from God to men or women. In this case, the Angel Gabriel visited Mary.

Luke 1:19

Gabriel also visited Zechariah to announce His Son's birth, later known as John the Baptist.

Mathew 1:20

An unnamed angel visited Joseph to assure him that Mary was still a virgin and carrying God's Son.

Has an angel called you with a message from God?

I have seen angels on several occasions and felt them at other times. I lived on Guam's island when someone from my church called to inform me my friend had an accident while diving in the ocean. She was at the military hospital. I immediately hopped into my car and drove through the rain toward the hospital, praying as I went.

I entered the gate. I heard: "Kathy has gone to heaven with the Lord."

I walked into the hospital room, where our minister and another friend sat. He came to me, hugged me, and crying, whispered: "She just died."

"I know," I said, "an angel told me."

To this day, I believe I heard an angel informing me of my friend's death.

Exodus 23:20

See, I am sending an angel ahead of you to guard you along the way and to bring you to the place I have prepared.

Another purpose I have noticed for angels is in our protection. I have often asked the Lord to send angels to surround my family and me during times of fear. I lived in Miami, Florida, during Hurricane Andrew. As the house fell around us and the air seemed to vacuum the room, I prayed: "Lord, please send your angels to surround our little area so that nothing will fall on us or take us away." Sure enough, the winds stopped shortly after that, and we escaped unharmed.

We lived in Egypt. My three children and I stood outside the zoo, waiting for our ride home. Rocks started flying around us. I looked back and saw local children throwing stones at us. I gathered the children close and prayed: "Lord, please surround us so the rocks will not hit." No rock hit us. Our ride arrived, and we went on our way.

I cannot say with certainty that these were not coincidences. I believe angels were stationed around us to protect us.

Mathew 18:10

See that you do not look down on one of these little ones. For I tell you that their angels in heaven always see the face of my Father in Heaven.

All-day, all night, angels watching over me, my Lord.

Does every Christian have a guardian angel?

Yes, I believe so. God tasked angels to watch over one human during that human's lifespan. When my first baby died, I saw a vision. A tiny angel stayed beside the baby wrapped in a blanket. Other angels lifted my son from one to the other up a ladder to heaven.

Colossians 1:16

For by him all things were created; things in heaven and on earth, visible and invisible, whether thrones or powers or rulers or authorities, all things were created by him and for him.

Prayer
Thank you, Lord, for your story of Christmas. Lift the veil of disbelief from the eyes of those who struggle to believe. Help them see the miracle and majesty of your Son, Jesus Christ, during this Christmas season.

"O Little Town of Bethlehem, How Still We See Thee Lie."

Luke 2:6-7

While they were there, the time came for the baby to be born, and she gave birth to her firstborn, a son. She wrapped him in cloths and placed him in a manger because there was no room for them in the inn.

Two thousand years ago, Bethlehem contained less than one thousand, but people obeying the census rules crowded the village at the time of Jesus' birth. Joseph sought room with relatives, but their guest rooms were full, so he found shelter in a stable.

To understand the culture of the time more fully, read *Some Wonderful Truths about the Night of Jesus' Birth According to the Bible and not Tradition*, Timothy A. Brown, December 7, 2013. https://goodnessofgodministries.international

Roman soldiers and officials were visible everywhere. The census could have taken days. Once counted, the people left, so Mary and Joseph could have moved to one guest room.

On the night of Jesus' birth, angels appeared where shepherds kept watch over their sheep.

Luke 2:8-9

And there were shepherds living out in the fields nearby keeping watch over their flocks at night. An Angel of the Lord appeared to them, and the glory of the Lord shone around them, and they were terrified, but the Angel said to them, "Do not be afraid. I bring you good news of great joy that will be for all the people. Today in the town of David, a savior has been born to you. He is Christ the Lord.

Angels we have heard on high, sweetly singing o'er the plain.

Two thousand years ago, people more easily believed in angels than we do today. The Christmas story is full of angels. Can you imagine how frightened the shepherds must have been when the night sky was ablaze in light with angels singing? The shepherds left their flocks with the boy watching over them and hurried down to Bethlehem so they could see the baby spoken about by the angels.

Can you imagine the shock on Mary and Joseph's faces when these strangers wandered in where they lay with the newborn child? What did Mary think? Joseph? Any doubt about their Son's parentage flew away, replaced with the knowledge God blessed them with His Son.

Imagine the shepherds as they returned to their flocks excited and telling everyone they met about their experience. What did those people think? The Bible does not say.

How long did Joseph, Mary, and Jesus stay in Bethlehem?

The Bible does not say. The carpenter, Joseph, could find work anywhere, but probably was anxious to return to Nazareth to his shop. Mary and Jesus were not ready for the trip home yet.

The Bible does not tell the time between Jesus' birth and the visit of the Magi. This event may have happened during the year of Jesus' birth or a year or so after.

What happened when Jesus was eight days old?

Luke records that Mary and Joseph took Jesus to the temple in Jerusalem when he was eight days old, so I think they went to Jerusalem from Bethlehem for this Jewish ceremony before the wise men arrived.

Luke 2:22

When the time of their purification according to the law of Moses had been completed, Joseph and Mary took him to Jerusalem to present him to the Lord and to offer sacrifice in keeping with what is said in the law of the Lord: a pair of doves or two young pigeons.

Jerusalem

Luke 2:21

On the eighth day, when it was time to circumcise him, he was named Jesus, the name the angel had given him before he had been conceived.

Being devout Jews, Joseph and Mary walked seven miles from Bethlehem to the temple in Jerusalem, where the priest circumcised and gave the baby the name Jesus. When he was 40 days old, they trekked back to the same temple for the purification ceremony prescribed by Moses's law.

The temple at Jerusalem, initially built in the 10th century BCE, destroyed and rebuilt by Herod, served during Jesus' time as the cultural and intellectual center for religious life. An older man named Simeon and a prophetess named Anna met the family on the temple grounds. Simeon took Jesus from Mary's arms and proclaimed:

Luke 2:29

Sovereign Lord as you have promised, you now dismiss your servant in peace for my eyes have seen your salvation which you have prepared in the sight of all people as a light for the reformation to the gentiles and for glory to your people Israel.

Suppose you brought your newborn to the temple or your church, and an old man and old woman known as the town's prophets were to say such a thing about your kid. What would you think? Mary and Joseph knew without a doubt that their Son was special and a gift from God, as are all babies, but Simeon told Mary a sword would pierce her heart. Food for thought.

NIV Luke 2:39

When Joseph and Mary had done everything required by the law of the Lord, they returned to Galilee to their own town of Nazareth.

What about the three kings (Magi)?

Tradition says they visited Bethlehem. The Bible does not.

Prayer
Thank you, Father, for sending your Son to us as we could learn to live our lives as you originally planned. May this Christmas bring peace to men and women and children of goodwill. In Jesus' name, I pray.
Adobe Stock
#1255

THE THREE KINGS, MAGI

Mathew 2:1

After Jesus was born in Bethlehem in Judea during the time of King Herod, Magi from the East came to Jerusalem and asked, "Where is the one who has been born King of the Jews? We saw his star in the East and have come to worship him."

Mary, Joseph, and Jesus were tucked away in a house. Joseph was a carpenter, and the boy was growing strong, healthy, and happy. He was probably a year or so old when the caravan carrying three kings or Magi arrived. The Magi had followed a star from Persia.

The Star of Bethlehem may have been a comet, or a planet, or a constellation.

The Magi (wise men) or kings studied the heavens and knew from reading their scriptures that a star would appear at the new King's birth. They charted their course and took a year of travel, always searching by the stars. When they reached Jerusalem, they spoke with Herod, who was the local king. They told Herod the time the star appeared and that this new King was born in Bethlehem.

Mathew 2:11

When coming to the house, they saw the child and his mother Mary, and they bowed down and worshiped him. Then they opened their treasures and presented him with gifts of gold and of incense and of myrrh.

Much happened during that first year of Jesus' birth. Traditions handed down through the centuries have changed a few of the Biblical details. However, the purpose is the same. God sent his Son, Jesus the Christ, to us for the salvation of our souls. That is why we, as Christians, celebrate Christmas: the birthday of our Savior.

Different cultures celebrate Three King Day.

December 25 is the beginning of the twelve days of Christmas and ends on January 5. Many cultures celebrate Christmas during those twelve days. January 6 is called Three Kings Day and the beginning of Epiphany.

Many Christians remove their Christmas decorations to signify the end of the Christmas season. People from different countries and cultures celebrate Three Kings Day with a delicious sweet cake. The round cake in Louisiana is filled with cinnamon, topped with white glaze, and sprinkled with purple, green, and gold sugar.

The person who finds a figure of baby Jesus hidden inside their slice of cake becomes "King" or "Queen" for the day. The Wise Men signify the non-Jewish people of the world. Three Kings Day represents a revelation of Jesus to the Gentiles.

How do you celebrate Three Kings Day?

Christmas Day

Isaiah 9:6

For to us a child is born, to us a son is given, and the government will be on his shoulders, and he will be called Wonderful Counselor Mighty God, Everlasting Father, Prince of Peace.

Wake up, world: it is Christmas Day. I am sure there is a white Christmas somewhere, but here, in Florida, the sun shines, the air is unusually cool, and birds swim on the lake behind my house. I walk into the living room, hoping to see signs Santa has visited, but I know that is not so. Our children have grown, and the grandkids are tucked away in their homes safe, warm, and secure. My husband and I sip our coffee, eat breakfast, and share greetings and simple gifts.

I want to join others today in a church service singing Christmas carols, but this pandemic Covid-19 and my recent knee surgery necessitate I stay secluded in my home. So, I search television for a church service and find none. The next best thing is to watch the Christmas marathon on Hallmark television. After several cartoons and movies, I note none of them invoke the "reason for the season."

What is the reason for the season?

The reason for the season is the same as it has been for two thousand years: to celebrate the birth of Christ. But no mention is made on television at all. The news talks of a detonation in Nashville, Tennessee, and the current death toll from Covid-19, only gloom and doom, not celebration.

The years 2000-2021 have been challenging for many.

The Covid-19 virus infected more than eleven million people or about ten percent of the worldwide population. The death toll exceeded two million. Every aspect of modern life has changed, leaving people in a state of uncertainty.

There is Hope.

Vaccines developed by pharmaceutical companies help fight disease, the plans developed by the governments help hurting people, and citizens share their homes, food, and concern with others. All is not lost. There is hope.

But what has this got to do with Christmas Day?

Christmas is the celebration of the birth of our Savior, Jesus Christ. He brought life, light, hope, and love into this dark world once ruled by Satan and man's sinful nature. Those of us who believe fear no evil, for God is beside us and within us. All we must do is open our hearts, minds, and pocketbooks to share our gifts with others. As I listen to Christmas carols and reread the greeting cards received, I recall those who have crossed my path and thank God for each one.

Prayer

Father, I hear there is now a mutated strain of Covid-19 that is more dangerous than the last. I pray you will aid nature in allowing this disease to mutate again into a less hazardous and possibly innocuous disease. In the meantime, help our scientists and health care personnel learn how to control the pandemic.

O Tannenbaum.
O Christmas Tree.

O Tannenbaum, O Tannenbaum,
O wee grün sind deine Blätter!
Du grünst nicht nur zur Sommerszeit,
Nein, auch im Winter, wenn es schneit
O Tannenbaum, O Tannenbaum,
O wie grün sind deine Blätter!

O Christmas Tree, O Christmas Tree,
How green are your leaves!
You grow not only in summertime,
No, also in Winter, when it snows.
Christmas Tree, O Christmas tree,
How green are your leaves?

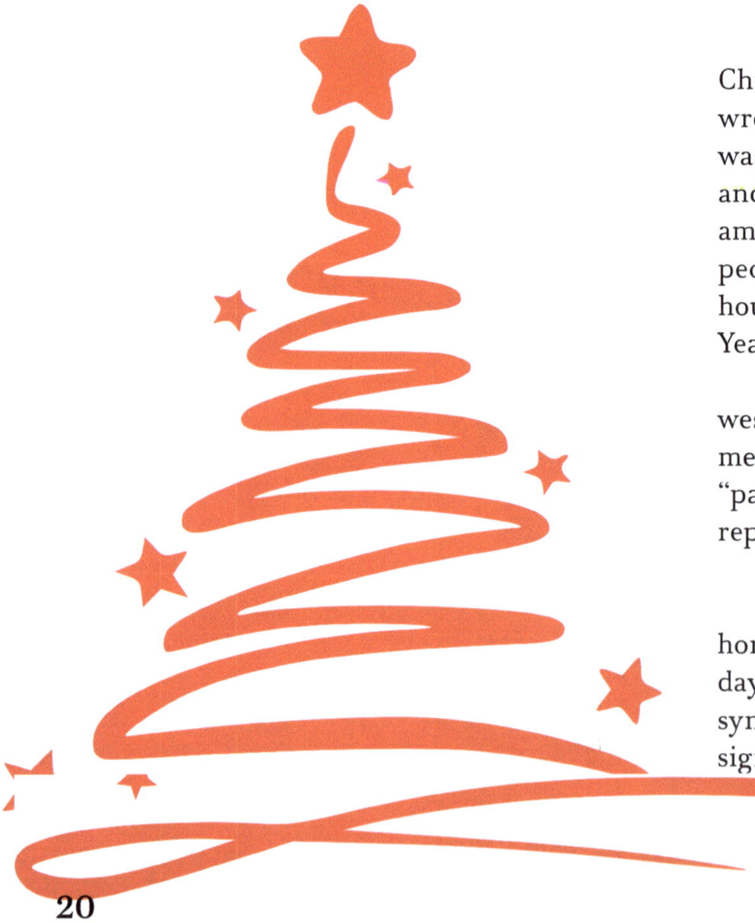

Jeremiah 17:7-9

But blessed is the man who trusts in the Lord, whose confidence is in Him. He will be like a tree planted by the water that sends out its roots by the stream. It does not fear when heat comes; its leaves are always green.

O Tannenbaum, taught in many elementary music classes and sung in most churches and Christmas carol groups, was written to honor fir trees but quickly adapted to celebrate Christmas trees. The first known Tannenbaum lyrics date to 1550 in Germany

When did the tradition of setting up a Christmas tree begin?

Like many customs celebrated by the Christian faith, the use of evergreen trees, wreaths, and garlands to symbolize eternal life was a custom of the ancient Egyptians, Chinese, and Hebrews. Tree worship was common among the pagan Europeans. In Scandinavia, people thought the tradition of decorating the house and barn with evergreens at the New Year scared away evil spirits.

The modern Christmas tree originated in western Germany. The main prop of a famous medieval play about Adam and Eve was a "paradise tree," a fir tree hung with apples representing Eden's Garden.

The Germans set up a paradise tree in their homes on December 24, the religious feast day of Adam and Eve. They hung wafers on it, symbolizing the eucharistic host (the Christian sign of redemption).

People often added candles symbolic of Christ being the light of the world. A Christmas pyramid or a triangular construction of wood decorated with evergreens, candles, and a star had shelves to hold Christmas figurines. It stood beside the tree. By the 16th century, the Christmas pyramid and the paradise tree had merged, becoming the Christmas tree.

How did the tradition of using various ornaments on a Christmas tree evolve?

The custom of decorating a Christmas tree emerged in the early 16th century when Martin Luther decorated the first Christmas tree with candles to entertain the children. During the 1800s, hand-cast glass ornaments became popular in Germany.

Christmas trees and fanciful decorations entered England in 1840 through Queen Victoria and her German Prince Albert. Ornaments reached America around 1880 when F.W. Woolworth imported them for sale.

Chrismon, meaning Christ monograms, are homemade, white, and gold designs made from Christian symbols signifying Christ. People often display them on an evergreen tree during the Christmas season in churches. Symbols such as crosses, fish, and the alpha and omega remind Christians of Christ's identity, story, and the Holy Trinity. Francis Spencer of the Ascension Lutheran Church in Virginia first developed these ornaments in 1957.

Share experiences you have had with Christmas trees.

When we lived in Germany, the people celebrated Christmas throughout December. Our neighbors set up a beautiful, evergreen tree with live candles. Splendid hand-carved ornaments hung from a Jesse tree nearby. An empty manger sat next to Mary in their nativity set. On Christmas Eve, our neighbor placed a baby doll in the manger. The Chirstkindl gave presents under the tree to the children.

On December 6, Saint Nicholas Day, my brother and I placed our shoes outside the apartment door. In the morning, we found both sticks and a chocolate bar in our shoes. St. Nicholas had visited and left them because we were both good and bad during the year.

We ate one candy cane each day from December 25th until January 1st, taken from the tree. We also received a paper book full of lifesavers from our grandfather.

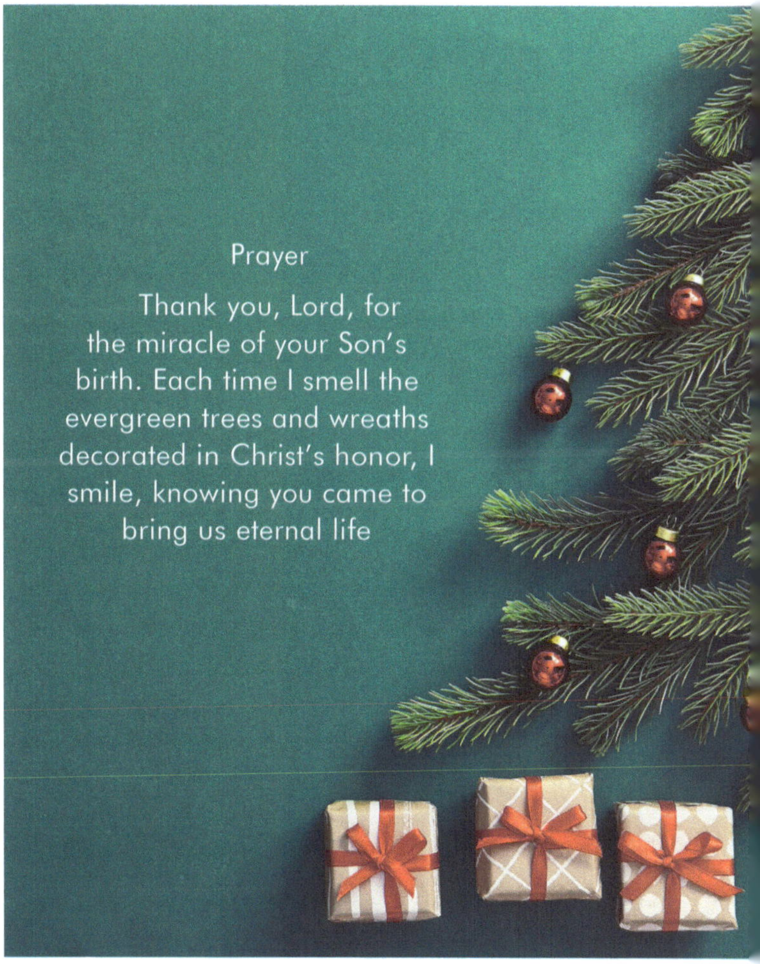
Prayer
Thank you, Lord, for the miracle of your Son's birth. Each time I smell the evergreen trees and wreaths decorated in Christ's honor, I smile, knowing you came to bring us eternal life

MERRY Christmas

Christmas Greetings

Luke 2:9-10

An angel of the Lord appeared to them (the shepherds), and the glory of the Lord shone around them, and they (the shepherds) were terrified. But the angel said to them, "Do not be afraid. I bring you good news of great joy that will be for all the people. . ."

On the night of Jesus's birth, angels sent the first Christmas greeting to shepherds watching their sheep. The shepherds immediately walked to Bethlehem and worshiped him in the stable where he was born.

Luke 2:17

When they had seen him, they spread the word concerning what had been told them about this child, and all who heard it were amazed at what the shepherds said to them.

Are you as amazed today as the shepherds were then or overtaken by commercialism and the story of Santa Claus?

After two thousand years of history, the knowledge of the life, death, and resurrection of this baby named Jesus, I still marvel at the grace God has shown us on this Christmas day. I am a Christian with complete faith in the word of God written and taught in the Bible. But what about those who are struggling with their faith or those who have no faith?

Hebrews 11:1

Now faith is the assurance of things hoped for, the conviction of things not seen.

Christmas has become a time of happiness, family gathering, and celebration for most Americans, Christian or not. Those of us of faith understand it is the celebration of the birthday of our Savior. We send greetings to all our friends, strangers on the street, and family, regardless of their faith. It is not a time to worry about converting non-Christians but rather a time of celebrating and, in so doing, perhaps, planting a few seeds of faith.

Americans mail 1.6 billion Christmas greeting cards a year.

People post more Christmas greeting cards, some containing family newsletters, than any other card during the year. Unique, handmade cards sold in specialty stores fill the postman's bag. Recently the tradition of sending greetings once a year is becoming a thing of the past, especially for younger people who post on Facebook or other social networks.

What is it like to receive a Christmas card each year?

Along with each year's Christmas card, I include a short newsletter with photographs informing friends and family of the important times we experienced during the year. When we receive a card, I always check the return address in case the sender has moved. I check first to see if a note or letter is enclosed, but I am often disappointed. Every year, fewer people are taking the time to write.

I am especially interested in sending individual cards to each child or grandchild. I recall the thrill of receiving an envelope addressed to me from grandma.

Just recently, I received an excited Facetime call from my son. His daughter yelled, "Grandma, we got your card." Each of the three young children took turns sharing their cards on-line with me.

Every nation celebrates Christmas in its traditions and language.

Regardless of the language, these greetings arrive in, whether Merry Christmas in English-speaking countries or Felis Navidad in Spanish, Joyeux Noel in French, Frohe Weihnachten in German, they all mean the same. "I am celebrating this season with you, someone I care about."

Prayer:
Thank you for the friends, family, and people you have sent into my life. May they find happiness and health during this Christmas season and in the new year to come. In Jesus' name, I pray.

С Рождеством
Craciun Fericit
Wesolych Swiat
Hyvää Joulua
Весела Коледа
Nadolig Llawen
Merii Kurisumasu
Joyeux Noël
メリークリスマス
С Рождеством
Craciun Fericit
Feli an Kristnaskon
メリークリスマス
Vesele Vánoce
Gëzuar Krishtlindjet
Glædelig Jul
Krismasi
Buon Natale
Buon Natale
Nollaig Shona
Selamat Natal
Feliz Navidad
Veselé Vánoce
Gëzuar Krishtlindjet
عيد ميلاد سعيد
عيد ميلاد سعيد
Buon Natale
Vroolijk Kerfeest
Feliz Natal
Merry Christmas
Hyvää Joulua
Mutlu Noeller
Wesolych Swiat
Kala Christouyenna
Merii Kurisumasu
Feliz Navidad
Весела Коледа
С Рождеством
Geseënde Kersfees
Nollaig Shona
Frohe Weihnachten
Glædelig Jul
Vroolijk Kerfeest
Joyeux Noël
Frohe Weihnachten
Mutlu Noeller
Nadolig Llawen
God Yul
Gleðileg Jól
Selamat Natal
Jwaye Nwèl
Bo Nadal
Jwaye Nwèl
Feliz Natal
Bo Nadal
Kala Christouyenna
Gleðileg Jól
Feliz Navidad
God Yul
Joyeux Noël
Frohe Weihnachten
Glædelig Jul
Krismasi
Geseënde Kersfees

Christmas Carols

Psalm 96:1
Sing the Lord a new song; sing to the Lord all the earth.

Music is as old as humanity itself.

A four-thousand-year-old Sumerian clay tablet contained the earliest musical notation with instructions on tunings for a hymn honoring the ruler Lipit-Ishtar. So, it is not unusual that the Bible records people and angels singing.

The Apostles sang songs from the Book of Psalms. The earliest known Christmas songs come from the 4th century. In the 12th century, St. Francis of Assisi introduced Christmas songs into church services. After Johannes Gutenberg invented the printing press, songs became more widely distributed.

Oliver Cromwell, who ended the British monarchy between 1649 and 1660, thought Christmas should be a solemn occasion. He abolished Christmas carol singing, but immigrants fleeing England brought the songs with them to the New World. In 1649, John de Brebeuf wrote the first American Christmas carol, called *Jesus is Born*.

The world's famous religious play, *The Passion Play*, of Oberammergau, Germany is performed every ten years since 1634. In the 1700s, the music by Mendelssohn and Handel was adapted and used as Christmas carols.

The first performance of Handel's *Messiah* occurred in 1742. By 1770 it was performed in Colonial America. Perhaps the best-known Christmas carol is *Silent Night*, written in 1818 by an Austrian assistant priest Joseph Mohr. The church organ broke the day before Christmas. Saddened, he sat down to write three stanzas that the choir could sing to guitar music. "Stile Nacht, Heilige Nacht" was heard for the first time at that Midnight Mass in St. Nicholas Church in Oberndorf, Austria. The congregation listened as the voices of Fr. Joseph Mohr and the choir director, Franz Xaver Gruber, rang through the church to Fr. Mohr's guitar accompaniment. Today, *Silent Night, Holy Night* is sung in more than 180 languages by millions of people.

Hark! The Herold Angels Sing.

Charles Wesley, brother of John Wesley, the Methodist Congregations' founder, authored more than 6,000 hymns. First published as a poem in 1739, this carol became one of the most beloved during Christmas time. Inspired by Luke 2:14, the song refers to the first time angels announced Jesus's birth to the shepherds. Whenever sung, this upbeat, happy announcement sounds over the airwaves.

Joy to the World! The Lord has Come!

Isaac Watts, an English hymn writer, wrote the lyrics based on Psalm 98 in the Bible. First published in 1719, it became one of the most sung hymns of all.

Away in a Manger, No Crib for His Bed.

First published in the late nineteenth century and used widely throughout the English-speaking world, it became the most famous melody. At first, the piece was thought composed by Martin Luther but revealed to be wholly American in origin.

What child is this, who, laid to rest, On Mary's lap is sleeping?

After suffering from illness and acute depression, William Chatterton Dix, in 1865, underwent a spiritual renewal leading him to write this poem set to the tune of Greensleeves. It is one of my favorites.

People continue writing Christmas Songs.

Mary, Did You Know?

A Christmas song addressing Mary, the mother of Jesus, lyrics written by Mark Lowry in 1984, and Buddy Greene in 1991, reached Number 6 on CCM Magazine's Adult Contemporary Chart. The song has since gone on to become a modern Christmas classic, recorded by hundreds of artists over the years across multiple genres. Different versions have reached the top ten in the Billboard R&B and Holiday charts.

What is the difference between a Christmas carol and a Christmas song?

Christmas carols are lyrics placed in a song related to the story of Jesus Christ, while Christmas songs are lyrics set in a theme related to the Christmas season. Most Christmas songs before 1930 were traditionally based on religion.

The Great Depression-era of the 1930s brought a string of Christmas songs about the holiday. These included *Santa Claus is Comin' to Town*, *Rudolph the Red-nosed Reindeer*, *Have Yourself a Merry Little Christmas*. *White Christmas* set the record of the most played Christmas song of the season. There is a more whimsical tune like *Grandma Got Run Over by a Reindeer*.

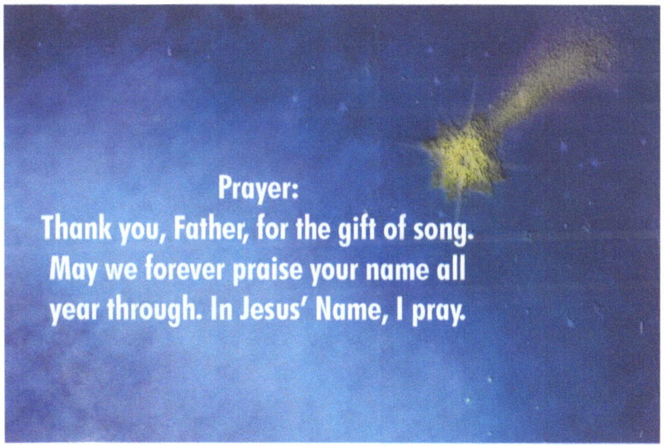
Prayer:
Thank you, Father, for the gift of song.
May we forever praise your name all
year through. In Jesus' Name, I pray.

We Wish You a Merry Christmas

Christmas Presents

Acts 20:35
It is more blessed to give than to receive.

How did giving gifts at Christmas begin?

During the middle ages, the Christmas celebration covered two weeks from Christmas Eve to the twelfth night or January 6. Between the 2nd and 8th century Christmas was a sober time of reflection and prayer. Often the Lord of the manor gave gifts of food and clothing to the people who served him.

Who started the idea of giving presents at Christmas?

A man born of wealth in Turkey in 280 AD became a Roman Catholic Bishop. People knew him as a generous man. In one recorded story, Nicholas sent three bags of gold down the chimney of a poor man's house, providing dowries for the daughters. The bags somehow landed in stockings hung by the fireplace. Miracles attributed to this famous saint include various healings and rescues of sailors and children. St. Nicholas became the patron saint of sailors and children as well as the first magical gift giver. On December 6, the anniversary of his death, parents, and friends give gifts to children.

The idea of giving Christmas presents, as we know it, started in England during the Victorian Era, about 1640. Gifts included food, cake, cookies, and fruit given to friends and family. This tradition evolved into the commercialization of Christmas.

Different gift-giving traditions spread through Europe. Kris Kringle delivers presents to well-behaved Swiss and German children, while The Chirstkindl is an angel-like figure often accompanied by St. Nicholas.

In Scandinavia, a jolly elf named Jultomten offers gifts in a sleigh drawn by goats. English legend explains Father Christmas visits each home on Christmas Eve to fill children's stockings with holiday treats.

Pere Noel fills the shoes of French children. Baboushka, an older woman who gave the wise men wrong directions to Bethlehem and later recanted, presents Russian children gifts on January 5th. In Italy, La Befana, a kindly witch who rides a broomstick down chimneys, delivers the presents.

Who is Santa Claus?

Immigrants brought their traditions to the New World. The name Santa Claus evolved from St. Nickolas' Dutch nickname, Sinter Klaas. Our Santa Claus comes from a poem, The Night Before Christmas, written by Clement Moore in 1822. The story was noted for his six children and published the following year anonymously. Santa Claus became a jolly older man dressed in red who rode a sleigh with eight reindeer. Children wait for him every Christmas Eve.

Are these traditions biblical?

No.

What were the first gifts given at Christmas?

Mathew 2:11

On coming to the house, they (the three wise men) saw the child with his mother Mary, and they bowed down and worshiped him. Then they opened their treasures and presented him with gifts of gold, frankincense, and myrrh.

Share with your family ways to give Christmas gifts during this season.

1. Anonymously pay someone's grocery or another bill.
2. Write a check to any worthwhile charity.
3. Give a gift to a shut-in or person in your neighborhood who has no immediate family.
4. Take an offering of dog and cat food to the nearest animal shelter.
5. Bake Christmas cookies and share them with a neighbor.
6. Purchase food at the grocery store for hungry neighbors.
7. Donate to Toys for Tots.

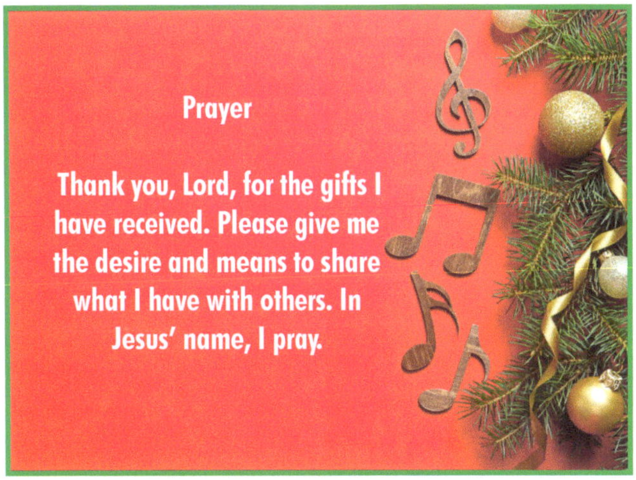
Prayer
Thank you, Lord, for the gifts I have received. Please give me the desire and means to share what I have with others. In Jesus' name, I pray.

Paper Plate Christmas Tree

Materials

1. Green paper plates
2. Tacky glue
3. Various materials for decoration
5. Scissors

Directions

1. Cut one paper plate in two.
2. Use ½ paper plate for one tree.
3. Fold half plate into a come
4. Staple the sides together to make the cone
5. Glue various decorating objects to the cone

Paper Plate Angel

Materials

1. White paper plate
2. Tacky glue
3. Gold Glitter
4. Gold Pipe Cleaner
5. Scissors
6. Round paper for face
7. Google eyes

Directions

1. Cut a deep triangle out of the paper plate
2. Place glue on the plate for wings
3. Sprinkle glitter over the glue
4. Glue triangle piece for the body
5. Make a face on round paper
6. Glue hair and eyes on the face
7. Glue body and face to the angel
8. Form halo from pipe cleaner
9. Tape halo to the back of the head

MERRY
Christmas

Christmas Puzzle Page

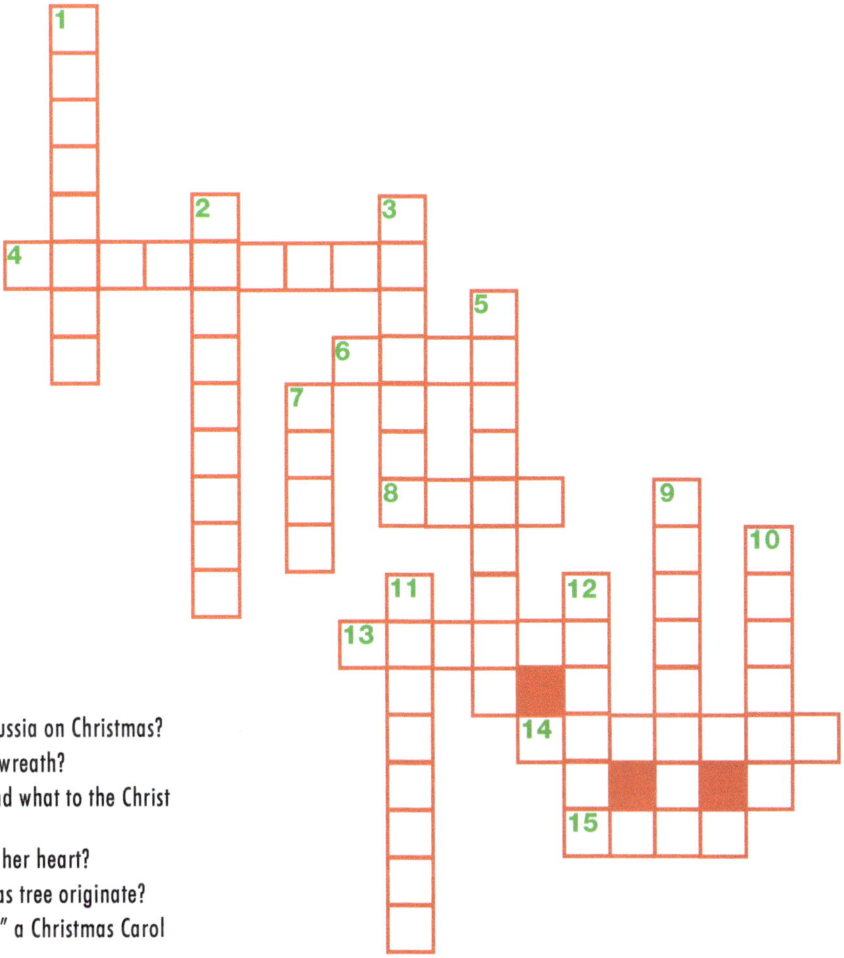

ACROSS

4. Who brings presents to children in Russia on Christmas?
6. How many candles are in an Advent wreath?
8. The Magi brought incense, myrrh, and what to the Christ child?
13. Who told Mary a sword would pierce her heart?
14. From where did the modern Christmas tree originate?
15. Is "Rudolph the Red-Nosed Reindeer" a Christmas Carol or a Christmas Song?

DOWN

1. Three King's Day begins what season in the church?
2. Who brings presents to children in Scandinavia?
3. Who was the greatest king of Israel?
5. Where was Jesus born?
7. Who was the mother of Jesus?
9. What are the white ornaments created in 1957 called?
10. What is the season of Christmas called?
11. Who was the first magical gift giver?
12. Who announced the birth of Jesus to the shepherds?

WORD BANK

Nicholas	David	five	Bethlehem
Chrismon	Jultomen	Germany	gold
Epiphany	Baboushka	Mary	Advent
angels	Song	Simeon	

Write Your Devotional Essays

How to Write a Personal Devotional

Writing a devotional essay is a fantastic way to share the insights and experiences you have during your Christian life. Focus on one word that shows a feeling or thought for the day. Use a concordance to establish a Bible verse that may connect with that word. Then write your experience in a short, concise passage connecting it with the verse. Engage the reader by connecting your interpretation of that verse to the experience. End with a prayer and a call to action to your reader.

Go ahead, think about today. What word comes to mind?

Love	Beginning
Beauty	Nature
Sorrow	Sin
Forgive	Church
	Worship

Now, look that word up in the Bible concordance.

Forgive, Forgave: Ps 32:5: Eph 4:32; Col 2:13; Col 3:13

Decide if the word you chose, like "Forgive," is about God forgiving you, you forgiving yourself, or someone else. It may be about your inability to forgive a wrong done to you.

Write one sentence telling God what is bothering you about that word.

Mary always says things that hurt me.

Then reread each verse and choose the one most appropriate to the situation.

Col 3:13
Bear with each other and forgive whatever grievances you may have against one another. Forgive as the Lord forgave you."

Now pray and think about how you can put the Bible verse into action.

It hurt me last night when Mary said________ __________________________. I did not respond, I just walked away, but now I cannot stop thinking about it. I want to call her up and shout at her, but I know that will do no good.

Time for Prayer

Write a short three-sentence prayer.

Father, thank you for giving me friends, even friends like Mary. Help me to understand why she is the way she is. Give me the strength, wisdom, and courage to forgive her for her transgressions and allow me to forgive myself for harboring any ill feelings toward her. In Jesus' Name, I pray. Amen.

It is time for a call to action to your reader.

Can you think of anyone who has wronged you in some way? If so, write a sentence about it, read scripture, write scripture, and pray for that person.

Collect these devotionals into a manuscript or notebook.

Decide if you wish to share them with people who may be struggling with the same situations you have, then find a publishing house, contact them for writer's guidelines and rework your devotionals to their specifications.

HAVE YOURSELF A MERRY LITTLE CHRISTMAS.

Christmas Scent

Christmas Recipes

"Everyone has their favorite Christmas and Holiday recipes. Here are three of mine."—
Peggy

Christmas Cranberry Smoothie

Ingredients:

1 cup almond milk

1 banana

½ cup frozen mixed berries

½ cup fresh cranberries

Directions:

1. Blend almond milk, banana, mixed berries and cranberries in a blender until smooth.
2. Refrigerate until chilled, at least 1 hour.

No Bake Sugar Cookie Bells

Ingredients:

¾ cup + 2 tbsp butter, softened

2/3 cup white sugar

1 Tbsp vanilla extract

1/8 to ¼ tsp almond extract

1 2/3 cup white flour.

Directions:

1. Beat together slightly melted butter with white sugar until well combined.
2. Add vanilla and almond extract
3. Beat in flour until well combined
4. Add flour ½ cup at a time
5. Roll perfect balls and refrigerate for 30 minutes
6. Split dough into equal parts and add food coloring. May also add sprinkles

Santa's Hot Chocolate

Ingredients:

4 cups milk

3 (1 oz.) squares semisweet chocolate, chopped

4 peppermint candy canes crushed.

4 small peppermint candy canes

1 cup whipped cream

Directions:

1. Heat milk until hot but not boiling
2. Whisk in the chocolate and the crushed peppermint candies until melted and smooth
3. Pour hot chocolate into four mugs, and garnish with whipped cream.

www.ingramcontent.com/pod-product-compliance
Lightning Source LLC
Chambersburg PA
CBHW050752110526
44592CB00002B/43

* 9 7 8 1 9 5 1 1 8 8 3 6 8 *